70 Amazing
Animal Collection

Amazing Animals Adult Coloring Book

Write a small brief about design.

Write a small brief about design.

Write a small brief about design.

Write a small brief about design.

Write a small brief about design.

Write a small brief about design.

Write a small brief about design.

Write a small brief about design.

Write a small brief about design.

Write a small brief about design.

Write a small brief about design.

Write a small brief about design.

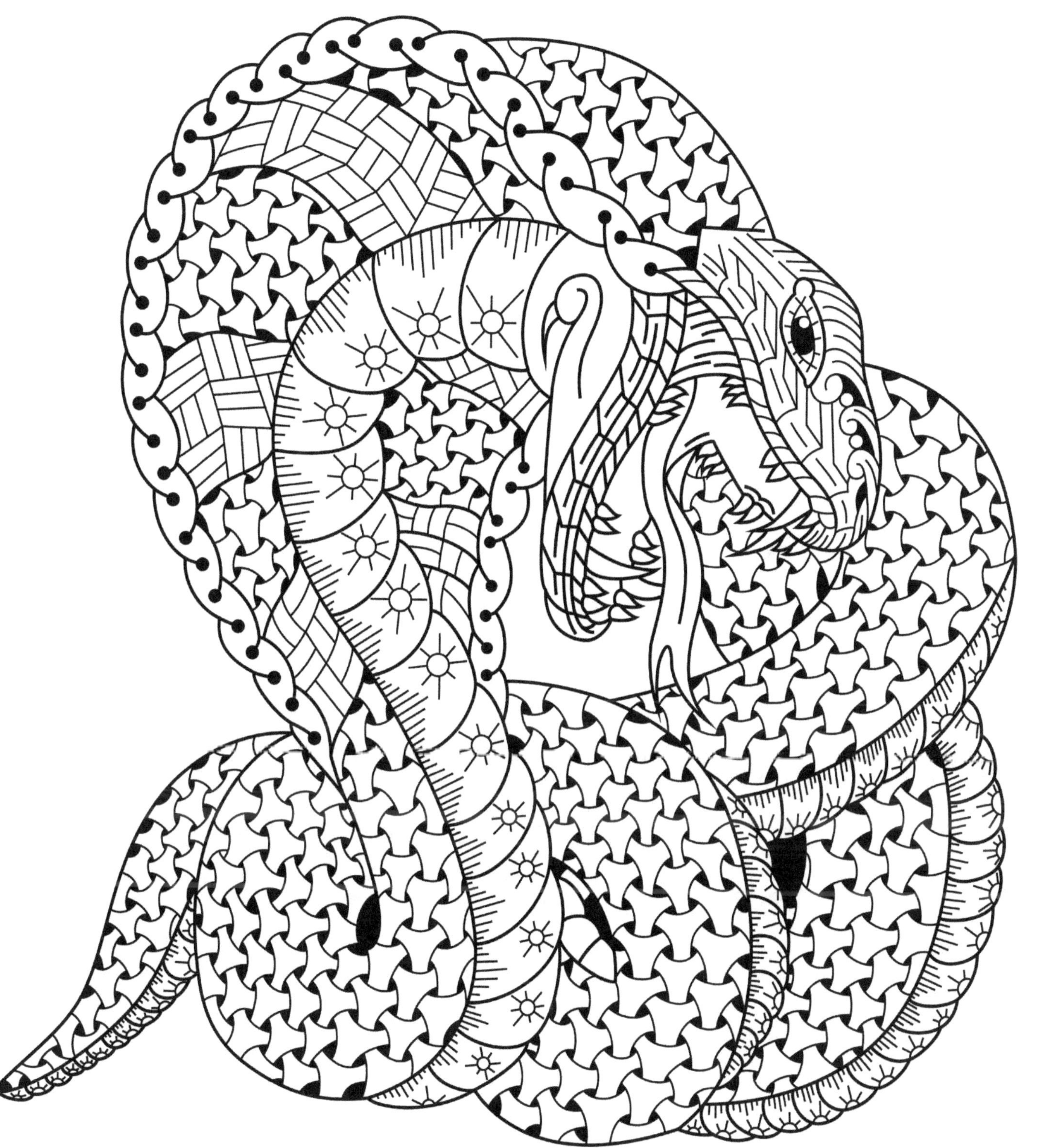

Write a small brief about design.

Write a small brief about design.

Write a small brief about design.

Write a small brief about design.

Write a small brief about design.

Write a small brief about design.

Write a small brief about design.

Write a small brief about design.

Write a small brief about design.

Write a small brief about design.

Write a small brief about design.

Write a small brief about design.

Write a small brief about design.

Write a small brief about design.

Write a small brief about design.

Write a small brief about design.

Write a small brief about design.

Write a small brief about design.

Write a small brief about design.

Write a small brief about design.

Write a small brief about design.

Write a small brief about design.

Write a small brief about design.

Write a small brief about design.

Write a small brief about design.

Write a small brief about design.

Write a small brief about design.

Write a small brief about design.

Write a small brief about design.

Write a small brief about design.

Write a small brief about design.

Write a small brief about design.

Write a small brief about design.

Write a small brief about design.

Write a small brief about design.

Write a small brief about design.

Write a small brief about design.

Write a small brief about design.

Write a small brief about design.

Write a small brief about design.

Write a small brief about design.

Write a small brief about design.

Write a small brief about design.

Write a small brief about design.

Write a small brief about design.

Write a small brief about design.

Write a small brief about design.

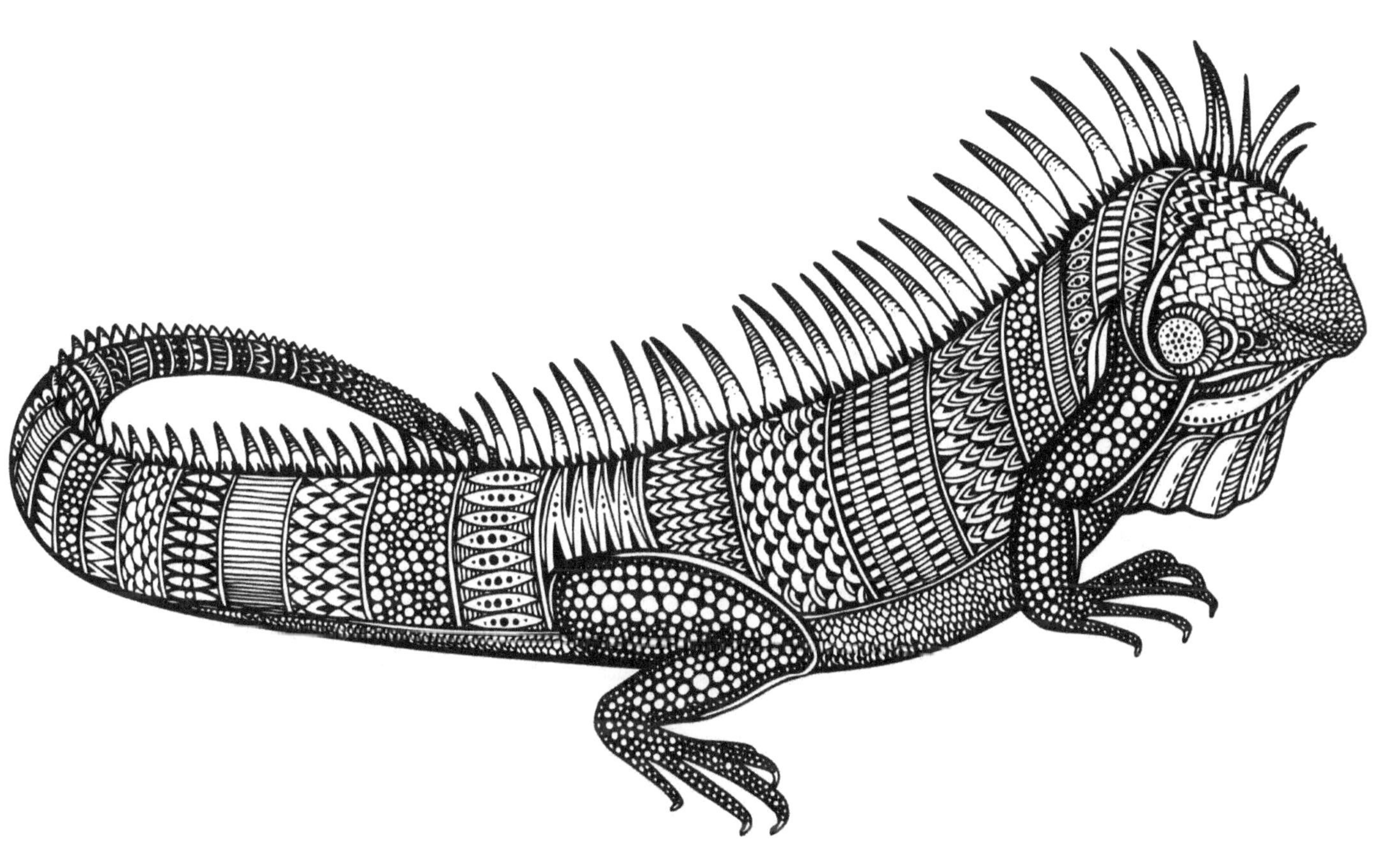

Write a small brief about design.

Write a small brief about design.

Write a small brief about design.

Write a small brief about design.

Write a small brief about design.

Write a small brief about design.

Write a small brief about design.

Write a small brief about design.

Write a small brief about design.

Write a small brief about design.

NOTE